TEXTBOOK OF A (PARENTHETICAL) LIFE: poems

RACHEL TOALSON

Other Books by Rachel

Poetry

This is How You Know
Life: a definition of terms
The Book of Uncommon Hours: haiku poetry
Textbook of an Ordinary Life
This is How You Fly
Sincerely Yours

Essay

Parenthood: Has Anyone Seen My Sanity?
The Life-Changing Madness of Tidying Up After Children
This Life With Boys
We Count it All Joy: Essays
Hills I'll Probably Lie Down On
If These Walls Could Talk
The Days are Long, But the Years Are Short
Life's Little Lessons: 100 Micro Essays

To see all the books Rachel has written, please click or visit the link below:

www.racheltoalson.com/writing

TEXTBOOK OF A (PARENTHETICAL) LIFE: poems

BATLEE PRESS

Published by
Batlee Press
Post Office Box 591596
San Antonio, TX 78259

Copyright ©2022 by Rachel Toalson
All rights reserved.
Printed in the United States of America.
Interior design by Toalson Media.
Cover design by Ben Toalson. www.toalsonmarketing.com

No part of this book may be reproduced or transmitted in any form or by any means, electronic or mechanical, including photocopying and recording, or by any information storage and retrieval system, without permission in writing from the publisher. For information regarding permission, write to Batlee Press, PO Box 591596, San Antonio, TX 78259.

The author appreciates your taking the time to read her work. Please consider leaving a review wherever you bought it and telling your friends how much you enjoyed it. Both of those help get the book into the hands of new readers, which is incredibly important for authors. Thank you for your support.
www.racheltoalson.com

Names: Toalson, Rachel, author.
Title: Textbook of a parenthetical life / Rachel Toalson
Description: First edition. | Batlee Press, Texas:
Batlee Press Books, 2022

10 9 8 7 6 5 4 3 2 1

First Edition—2022

For Mom
Thank you for working so hard
loving so fiercely
believing so steadfastly

Introduction

If there is anything I have come to understand in my life, it is this: Sometimes days stretch endlessly into a mundane calendar of to-dos, which makes the years fly by without any distinguishable accomplishment. Sometimes it feels like we are stuck inside some kind of waiting room and it's locked, barred, and practically impenetrable.

That's where this book came from: the rote days of motherhood, the endless days waiting for a career to take shape (I am still waiting), the disappointing days of feeling like you're going absolutely nowhere—how long will it take to get somewhere?

That's what a parenthetical life is: It's the life between the big moments. It's the tiny little things that only get bigger, more significant, when looking back, from the other side of the parentheses. It's the holding area, the waiting room, the pause button that makes us invisible—or seemingly so.

But really, the parenthetical life is just as important as the life outside the parentheses, the beginning and the end. The middle is all about the journey. It's the place we learn, finally, that life isn't so much about the origin or even the destination; it's about all those places in between. The steps we took between point A and point B. The hoping, the anticipation, the work of living.

These poems may have been written in a parenthetical

place, but they became so much more—a path to awakenings I am still unpacking today.

As I've said before (and will say again), you may not always agree or feel comfortable with my words or the place I land in my poems. But please don't let that stop your reading. I don't know everything, have never claimed to. These parenthetical years have changed me, but I am not done growing, learning, becoming.

We never are, are we?

I hope you find joy, love, and inspiration in the pages that follow.

Peek

I love
reading a book
in which someone

has handwritten
their observations
and thoughts in the margins;

it is like taking
a peek into
another person's life.

An Ode to Poetry

When I am ecstatic
poetry is my greatest
expression

When I am bowed by sorrow,
it is in poetry that I find
the courage to carry on

When I am
confused
poetry clarifies

When I am overly satisfied
poetry shows me I have
miles to go before I sleep

When I am tired
poetry says
Let us do our work as well

When I cannot walk
for the heaviness in my soul
poetry calls
Be strong!

When I am overcome
with aloneness poetry posits
it has been here before
when *I wandered lonely as a cloud*

When I criticize myself
for despicable thoughts
poetry whispers
The quality of mercy is not strained

When I have lost my grip
on faith poetry assures
In what a forge and what a heat,
Were shaped the anchors of thy hope!

When I am curious
poetry opens new
unexamined worlds

When I feel fear
poetry lights
the way

When the darkness
crowds corners, poetry
magnifies the sun

The Masters

To write like the masters—

this is what I
aspire to do

to share in their
taming of language

their sense of
rhythm

their lofty
examination—

but then I take out
my poet's pen and I can think

of nothing else to examine
but the masters:

what they have already achieved.

Black Pen

They are slipping and sliding
    all over the floor
in socks put on for this purpose
    Slip, slide, slip, slide
until one of them falls
    and scrapes a knee
or an elbow
    or a mouth

And sometimes this is what
    talking feels like—
all over the place
    thoughts like errant birds
darting through my mind
    I'm unable to capture one
long enough to shape it
    into a coherent thing to say
I grasp, but the words
    are predictably out of reach
He asks me what I think;
    I cannot, in all honesty, say

But the world becomes clear
    the moment I pick up
my pen and write

    All those thousands of thoughts
rearrange into a beautiful
    clarity of consciousness
and I am struck by how words
    can progress from
slippery little things
    to large, graspable pieces
all because of a
    black pen

Writer

sometimes I find myself
thinking that this was a life
made for someone else
that I am not the right
person to live it
sometimes I forget my song
and how to sing it
sometimes I wonder at my
abilities or lack thereof
do I have what it takes?
can I do what must be done?
is this right for me?

no one answers
those particular questions

there are others that gnaw
at my sides and
aim their swings
and spread their poison
until my skin burns
and my feet falter
and my eyes close in exhaustion
(or is it simply surrender?)
and I begin to think

I have my answer—
yes, of course
this is all too much
no, of course I don't
have what it takes
no, of course this is not
my life to claim
it is not right for me
it is completely
and utterly wrong

I want to give up on those days
I want to put away my pen
and close my notebook and
find a simpler less tortured life
but something always keeps me
something always holds
it is the generous act of writing

pouring
    thoughts
        dreams
            emotions
        people
    out on a page

without it I would shrivel up

into less than myself
and I have been there before
I don't want to
be there again

and maybe I won't ever be
number one or
even number two
or number ten or
number one hundred
it's not the numbers
that count so much
it's the sustainable work of it
the every-day living
and breathing and doing
and I live and breathe and do
which means I am
exactly where I
need to be

I have been writing relentlessly
for eight thousand
three hundred
seventy-five days

White Space

Why am I
so dry of words?

I sit down to write something

      as I always do
      every day
      religiously

and the words,
the finding of them,
feel impossible—

is it exhaustion,
disappointment,
pressure?

The world is heavy
when I cannot
write.

All I want to do
is craft a poem,
profound or otherwise,
but all I can manage to

see

hear

feel

taste

touch

is white space.

Transcendent

There is something
transcendent about poetry

Some complain that they can't
understand what poets are trying to say

because the poems are melodramatic
and poets often speak

in metaphor and
mystery

I wish they could see how poetry
brings a world to life

how poetry whispers
possibility

how poetry takes a knotted up picture
and smooths it out clear

So maybe one has to look deeper
than the surface to see what's there—

but it's only in poetry that

we empty the private spaces

through poetry that
we are known and loved

with poetry that
we rise above the earthen realm

and touch the hand
of our creator

To Life

I write because I have to—

that's what we usually say
because if we don't write
it would feel like dying

but the truth is I write
because I need to
because without writing

I would not be able to breathe
or smell or hear or see
or feel or know

or at least I would have
no memory of it
so what writing does at its heart

is make my world clear and
preserve for me the memory of a moment
that will last forever and ever

tonight it's my kids in the hallway
giggling and cutting up and rough-housing
even though they should be in bed—

rather than storm out my bedroom door
with a fury that might be devastating
I pick up my pen and

write my way back into life

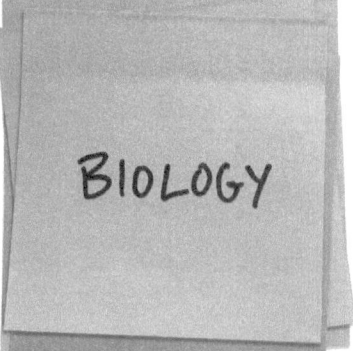

The Vanishing Roads

The song of winter
lingers for but a moment
its last note of longing
ringing strong and wild
and cold and then
like a masterpiece that is
heard but not quite seen
it wets the way
for spring flowers and
              vanishes

The spring flowers bloom
lending their reds and
purples and yellows
to a world that is
brand new but not quite
proving the extravagant beauty
winter can hide
giving us a spectacular view
on the sides of highways
where we might stop to snap
whimsical family pictures if we so desire
and then the hot summer wind exhales
and the spring flowers fold up and
              vanish

The hot summer wind lifts hair
from the napes of our necks
and kisses our checks
with bursts of delight and
moves out upon bodies
invisible yet present
coaxing flies from their hiding places
sending overheated grandparents indoors
bending trees in their trunks so we can
see and understand its power
and then the whole world
stills and it
                vanishes

Fall whistles through treetops
        cuts across canyons
                sneaks into backyards
where children lift faces to the sky
shout, *Fall's here!*
rush inside to light candles
that smell of apple and
pumpkin and cinnamon
joining the scents of baked goods
        pies cakes spiced cookies
treats for later
but much too soon

the wind turns and
the colorful leaves
succeed in their
                vanishing

We are born into
light and wonder
discovering the mystery of seasons
basking in the warmth of love
uncovering the layered
diamond of life and then
we grow wrinkled and bent
and weak and
like the song of winter
the spring flowers
the hot summer wind
the scents of fall
we too
                vanish

The Storm

the clouds hunch low
blotting out the sun
curling white at the edges
but gray all over their massive middles

they burst with the promise
of a summer storm
and as I watch
I wonder

how do I survive this
how do I carry on
how can I do
what has been asked of me

meeting a woman
meeting her children
meeting a man who
traded me for them

how can one
even ask
how can a world
hold

so much hatred
so much turmoil
so much
storm

it was only yesterday
that I played in the warmth
watched my brother
roller blade

down the sidewalk
soaring over the ramp
he'd made out of
Memaw's old table

she looked on from the porch
we tried not to think
about what would come tomorrow
on a day as perfect as that one

but time does not
stop marching for those
who are unready
no time hurries on

the moment we awoke
we could feel the rain

that would fall later
and we were right

it frosted our faces
chilled our arms
bittered our hearts
that had to embrace

a baby's cry—
one who did not belong
a girl's voice—
another who did not belong

the storm had bleached hair
and dark brown brows
and a ring
all too familiar

that storm blew
the whole day dark
so we could
hardly see

up from down
in from out
right from left
right from wrong

years passed and did what
all years do—
poured rain
and flashed sun

and it was only once a heart
had endured both
that it could sing its
deep song and be heard:

though we may be tempest-tossed
we are still standing

Water

Water falling
in heavy drops
from the sky

darkening the pavement
spotting his backpack
while he talks to a friend

and I try to keep up
my toes blistering from
the constriction of new shoes

I wish I could take them off
but restraint grits my teeth
and walks me on

Water glistening
beneath the bridge
sending back to me

a reflection of the
buildings that are
lit up and loud

and as we pass

I pause for a moment
peer over the edge

but not too far for fear that
I'd careen over the bar
with someone's ill-timed joking push—

and then I would lose my work
which is strapped to my back
and maybe even my life

Water nearly white
in a glass tub
cubed ice crackling in it

I angle my bottle
beneath it and as soon as
I turn it on some splashes

to the floor in
large splatters
a pool of invisibility

By the time my bottle fills
it dries and the water is gone
soaked up into cloth and wood

Eye

One eye peering out at her from behind a limb.
One eye fastened on her from the corner of the bar.
One eye telling her she would be nothing.
One eye laughing at the spectacle she'd made.
One eye watching her vision in white.
One eye believing she could be everything.
One eye peering out at her from behind a limb.

Imaginative Assumptions

Observation

i

My husband has been acting strangely. I can't say exactly how; perhaps it's my imagination. He is distracted, mostly —paying more attention to his phone than to me, as if the conversation is more scintillating on a screen. When he leaves his phone on his bedside table to go shower, I want to pick it up. I want to search it. I want to find what steals his attention.

Who is she?

ii

He is staying out late. He is evasive about where he needs to be. He has more meetings than he used to. When he comes into our room, while I am working, he is always on the phone.

Where did he meet her?

iii

He needs a hair cut, he says.

Why? I say.

His hair is getting out of hand, he says. You know how it gets.

I thought you liked your long hair, I say.

I thought you didn't, he says.

He's right. I don't. It's never mattered before; I'm not pushy about it.

What does she look like?

Reflection
Reflecting on all the facts,
    I can't help but assume that
        he has found greener pastures
Elsewhere
    perhaps she is younger and can unfold like a
Flower, the way I used to. Perhaps she
Loves him better than I
Essentially could. Love is easier
    in the beginning, more exciting, profound.
    We have grown distant, apathetic. When you're
Crazy about each other, every kiss,
    every touch feels like you're standing
    in the middle of a fire
That nothing could extinguish, and maybe

I should have been something more to him.
    Maybe I should check up
On it, maybe I don't really want to know
    that there is someone else he's been
    meeting in some
Noxious place that doesn't have a soul,
    which is how I feel right now.

Experimentation

I check his phone, but I find nothing. I dig deeper about the meetings, but he is noncommittal. I sign off on the haircut as No Big Deal. I wait for the confession.

He shows up at the door in his skinny jeans and a blue shirt that makes his eyes glow, offers his hand, and surprises me with a rare night out, sans children.

All planned furtively.

Hurricane

for Hurricane Harvey, which hit Texas August 17, 2017

Sight
Trees twisting in a wind you can never see, a ghost blowing through green. Rain falls in sheets, obscuring houses from one another. The gray sky is the largest expanse visible, a frowning face on all that has passed through here, and, perhaps, all that has yet to come.

Sound
Wind howls down the canyon, the same way it does when a cool front blows through. It sounds almost hopeful, except that rain slams against the window, a steady rhythm to the cadence of the movie my children are watching to take their mind off the monster outside, at least until the power goes out.

Smell
The air is salty, like spray off the ocean. The rain turns everything musty and old, ancient drops recycling through clouds and earth. In my house I am arranging chocolate chip cookies on a plate, comfort food. My husband's familiar scent of spice and tweed reaches for me. I reach back.

Taste

A metallic flavor coats my mouth, the taste of fear twirling on my tongue, stoking a fire in my chest, as I wait to hear from family who stayed behind, hoping their presence in their homes might somehow dissuade the wind from lifting off roofs and tearing down walls, the rain from soaking yards and rooms in dangerous capacity.

Feel

The power is the most surprising. I stand, for a moment, out on my back deck, braving the gusts. It wants to pull me along, perhaps lift me in the air so I can dance, become Mary Poppins sailing on an umbrella, but I resist, flee back inside, slam shut my door, feel the cool white wood stick to my forehead while my heart trips over forbidden possibilities.

Leaves

In them
you can see the veins of life,
spidering toward the edges,
curling up at the ends,
dry, beaten, torn in places
like they have been used up
to their fullest.

And now that they have been
used up to their fullest,
they will become
part of the
forest floor.

And one day
we will join them,
the circle of life
spiraling on.

The Dawn

It hides in the
splash of a surprise,
in the gentle breath
of morning that
billows out in a cloud
that is here one moment,

gone the next,
as if it, too, understands
the promise of daybreak.
It is a tender awakening,
a shake on the shoulder,
a kiss on the cheek,

ushering in a gentle morning
so welcome, so bright
after a dark night,
and though the eve
can be lovely with its
white moon and silvery stars

it is not quite so lovely
as the dawn, which holds,
in its magnificence,
the power to begin

the world
anew.

HEALTH SCIENCE

Laughter

it is magical
           this laughter
or perhaps medicinal
able to take
a man's shriveled up heart
a woman's torn up life
and mend it with

           a giggle a shake a silence

that only tells its secret
with the watering of eyes

and when it is shared
it can walk across valleys
and pull down walls and
bridge every gap
between love and hate

it is astounding that laughter
is not welcomed as
the miracle it could be

the world could use
more laughter

the world could use
more people laughing
the world could use
           a miracle

laughter remains
in even the hardest places
because

      it is the impossible
      the failed trying
      the never-evers
that need it most

Phone Call

1
I am sitting in my car
       sitting in my car
              sitting in my car
while the world's people live their lives
right outside my window
I can't join them, because, you see
I am different than I was yesterday
       and, also, I am terrified—
             too terrified to speak my pleasantries
to the ones who have not
known this terror

2
I am standing at my desk
       standing at my desk
              standing at my desk
trying to keep it together
trying to get a handle on the
hot rush of emotion that
weakens my legs so I can't stand
       can I stand I sure can't write
              may as well give up now
because of a stupid phone call
that invited this terror into my life

3
I am eating at my table
      eating at my table
           eating at my table
it's all surreal—their voices
their lack of concern for this
terror that covers me in a
cold wet suffocating blanket
      I don't say a word
           I don't even eat
who could when the world
has grown small—dark—unsafe—

4
I am lying in my bed
      lying in my bed
           lying in my bed
and don't I know I won't be
sleeping tonight my mouth
is too dry this can't be happening
why God why me
      I don't even know what to say
           or do or think I'm so angry
so shocked so terrified
what does anyone do with

it could be cancer

The Anatomy of a Migraine

You spend all day at the zoo.

It's a beautiful day
not a cloud in the sky
The air is perfect
a chill of fall peeking out
from the corners
They are all on their
best behavior for
at least the first half hour

But it gets to you after a while—
the sun the breeze
the watching over them all
to make sure no one gets lost
the perfume of other people
other people

You can feel it coming on
It starts surreptitiously
right between your
shoulder blades
a small spot of tension
By noon it's climbed up
your neck and the back

of your head

You don't even
realize until you're in the car
and everybody's crying
about how they
don't want to go home
that you must have been
clenching your jaw for at least
the last hour because your
jawline and ears and cheeks
feel sore like someone has
taken a bludgeon to your face
You can't see straight
your heartbeat magnifies
in your ears
their voices do the rest.

There are two more stops—
the library and a pizza place—
and the ache moves to the spot
between your eyes
soaking everywhere it's
already touched
You try to decode words
see their faces
talk to them at the very least

but your temples feel like
they weigh much more
than your neck can carry
You would like to go home
make the world dark and silent
sleep

You try to read to them
for their evening story time
but the pain worsens
becomes so colossal it's now
dripped into your stomach
It's too much; you'll either
throw up or pass out
and neither would be favorable
so you excuse yourself to lie down
missing out on the evening routine
hoping he does not resent you
for this excusing

Your head feels as though
it is being rhythmically pressed
between steel claws
like it has plans to
squash out your brains and
leave you a puddle on the floor—
pulsing radiating pain so intense

you can no longer hold yourself up
with your own two legs

So you sleep instead
and hope that in the morning
it will be gone

Alone

alone—

> with silence all around
> the fringes and
> widening in the middle

alone—

> without a single person depending on me
> so if I want to go to bed
> without eating dinner at all
> or if I merely pour myself a bowl of cereal
> I could do it without consequence

alone—

> I could slip beneath
> the covers of my bed and
> between the pages of a book
> and read until the early gray of morning
> presses at the corners of curtains

alone—

> I could open a notebook
> and finish a full thought
> before it's gone from me
> flown away on an imaginary wind

alone—

    I might stare at the lights
    and remember what it's like
    to wonder

alone—

    no overwhelming voices
    no invading touches
    no constant activity of
    flitting from one thing to another

alone—

    a luxury I would enjoy
    for only a few minutes
    before alone became
        lonely

It's About My Skin

the sun

grows a flower
feeds a plant
controls the year

grants vitamin D
regulates body temperature
boosts mood

and yet I am afraid of
the sun

Words I Remember

why are you always pouting girl / doesn't your mother / teach you how to greet / your life with gratitude / without complaining / like a decent human being / she's too soft on you / you're all going to grow up / to be ungrateful human beings / complaining about what life throws your way / well let me tell you / life throws some / crazy stuff your way / you better just get used to that / starting with me and your mom / you know shit happens / so stop your pouting / wipe that look off your face right now / don't you start crying / I'll give you something to cry about / I'll —

why do I always become a little girl in his presence?

A Question

The question is what gets me the most:
What do you want?
           I don't know—I want everything.

I want the easy life
but I want the expert life
         and can I have both?

I want the calm mind
but I want the creativity
         and can I have both?

I want money
but I want to focus only on what I love doing
         and can I have both?

I want children
but I also want to remember who I am
         and can I have both?

I want notoriety
but I also want out of the spotlight
         and can I have both?

I want my days filled with laughter

but I also want times of silence
               and can I have both?

I want space
but I also want to be held
               and can I have both?

I want ease and comfort
but I also want challenge and growth
               and can I have both?

I want to find myself
but I also want to lose myself
               and can I have both?

What do I want?
Everything, but maybe that means
               I am dangerously close to wanting

nothing

Describing

Reasonable
I try to be reasonable. When my children do things they're not supposed to or my husband isn't as considerate as I expect or someone walks all over me online—I try to shake it off. I'm a nice person, don't lose my patience or decorum often.

But push me over that edge, and you'll see just how unreasonable I can be.

Anxious
He didn't come home when he said he would. So now I'm examining a handful of possibilities in my head—maybe he ran off, maybe he's with another woman, maybe he's on the side of the road, dead, in which case I need to make a plan for supporting my family alone on a writer's salary, which is to say, on practically nothing.

Never does the logical explanation come calling—that he simply had something else to do and forgot to tell me before his phone died.

Congenial
In any conversation I try to find a point of similarity—a shared interest, experience, opinion. I listen for the

nuances of story, for the hidden pieces of a person, to find where we are alike.

The art of good conversation lies in congeniality.

Human
In spite of the differences in our physical appearances, in the foreign nature of our upbringings, in the passionate opinions we share or don't, we all want the same things. Love, hope, beauty, kindness, a place to belong.

At our simplest, we are all the same: human.

Enigmatic
When I hear someone say I'm mysterious, I always want to laugh—have they read nothing I've written?

I live quietly, but I write loudly.

Large
I want to live a large life. I have a large family. I have always worked hard to avoid a large body. When I was eleven years old I tried to do exercises from Judy Blume's *Are You There, God? It's Me Margaret* to make my breasts large. Sometimes my body craves a large salad. When I was three, my father seemed large to me, and every time I see him now I'm shocked by his averageness. One of the most

annoying things, in my opinion, is a large pimple the day before pictures. A large slice of homemade pie is the best reward for the end of the week. What will it take to live a large life?

A Learning

I have a propensity for drama
                or so I've been told
when I was young
I would cry
at the least little thing

a stray dog on the side of the road
                hit by a too-fast car
a small girl in a wheelchair
an old man leaning against
his caregiver, talking gibberish

they all called forth great emotion in me
so I could not look at them
                without weeping
and the ones who called me dramatic
could not see my tears without
thinking them unnecessary

and so I grew up biting my lip
swallowing my sadness
turning away when
the emotion rose too high in my throat
because a dramatic child is one thing
                but a dramatic adult

no one wants to be that

I learned to hide myself
behind sheets made of brick
thick and tall and indestructible
until one day
           they proved destructible

because one day I sat
in a room with three women
talking about my son
           my son who is kind
           my son who is beautiful
           my son who is brilliant
                      and wise and good
as they told me about
his self-harm threats his sadness his failures
in a place where it mattered
I felt my walls trembling
           I tried to turn away
but they crumbled anyway
me with them

years of sorrow
years of hiding
years of trying to be
           other than who I was

and I folded in front of strangers
and yet it was the bravest I had ever been

because in the sorrow I sought answers
in the seeking answers I found solutions
in the finding solutions I found me

              whole complete weak
              and yet so strong

and I learned then
that the stronger our weakness
              the wiser we become

is that not worth something

Family and Child Development

Mastery

they are them
    ducking under tables
    shouting in a crowded room
        about nothing and everything
        all at once
    dipping fingers into icing
    to smear a smile
        across their face
        and it is not love
    it is not anything close to love
    that fans the fire raging inside
        that strikes a hand
        and watches words
    the way a child waits
    which is to say
        not at all

it is not anything close to love
    that balls up tight
    like a dark stone stomping out
        all the tenderness that might
        once have been there
    but then again maybe not

and you'd think

you'd think after all these years
after all these wrinkles
    etched in a brain
    after all this wisdom earned
and this imagination unleashed
and the both together
    working to make me
    a real woman
you would think I'd learn

but today it's the same old story
    again and again and again
    grasping love but not quite
        because you see
        it is not the workings of a mind
    that give one this genius
    it is the workings of a heart
        and there is not warmth enough today
        to set me on that height
    because they are them
and I am me

I am me
    and they are them

why is it so hard
    to love who they are today

      when did love become
           this aching impossibility
           this slick serpent
      this thing made entirely of flight
      when brown eyes turned opportunistic
           when hands chose hiding
           when lies began to thrash
      a tender past and
      the longest distance
           between there and here—
           that is, the scar
grew longer

I don't know

all I really know is
    love
    life's greatest genius
        feels like a fading star
        a child today has not
    the unconditional acceptance
    of his mother

I am his mother
    I do not unconditionally
    accept him today
        I am his monster

        in a forest of experimentation

I want this genius
    need it so desperately
    but the only movement it makes
        from one day to the next
        is up toward higher ground
    farther away than I can reach

yet I press on
    ever reaching for the
    slippery limbs of love
        because I know
            someday
        someday
    someday
    it will come to me willingly
        and I will have mastered
        too
this genius

Daughter

she was pink

>	new
>	untouched
>	unknown

it is all
she would ever
>	be

Motherhood in Eight Parts

i

He came into the world fighting, and it was how he would live in it, too, grappling his way to the last word, changing everything, taking rules and flipping them on their heads at the least hint of inconsistency, and in his fighting, in his always challenging the status quo, he showed me that life can be an adventure in the opposite direction, that treasure can be found in the most imperfect places (even in me), that questions can forge a better, truer, brighter world.

ii

He slid into the world so easily, so eagerly, so rapidly he had marks from the journey in red splotches all over his face and neck and arms, and it was the way he would walk all his days, easy, eager, rapid, because there was wonder in even the smallest of things, and his exuberance taught me to see the newness in every bit of old, to appreciate the surprise of the unknown, to find joy in the most tedious pieces of life (even laundry) because it was a gift.

iii

He came to us wide-eyed with curiosity, and it was how he'd find his place, peering into closets, attempting stairs before stairs were safe, shadowing the ones who could do everything he wanted to do, and in his risking, in his exploring, in his falling down and getting back up, he showed me that a life was meant to be danced with risk and courage and abandon.

iv

He slipped into our lives minutes before his brother, and it was how he would do everything, one step ahead, one plan ahead, one mischievous act ahead, and in his planning, in his figuring out, in his always trying, never giving up, he taught me that perseverance can be spread across every circumstance (especially the most undesirable), because there is always a way—even where the opposite seems true.

v

He was the second to appear with an immediate scream that told us all was well, and it was the way he would move about his environment, pointing out the injustice, communicating exactly what it was he wanted, not resting until he had the right materials, the right opportunities, the right setup, and what he taught me with his inflexibility, his dogged pursuit, his single-minded focus is that sometimes it is okay to fight for the little things.

vi

He wasn't quite ready for the world, but he came willingly, because it was time in the grand scheme, and it was how he would walk his days, ever ready, choosing joy, imparting delight at every turn, and in his smile, in his laughter, in his pulling away and always returning to the arms of safety, I learned that there are simple pleasures in life that have nothing to do with circumstances and everything to do with the lenses we wear.

vii
Motherhood has taught me how to become myself, how to accept myself, how to care for myself.

viii
Love begins and ends here.

Invisible

invisible

is the name I wear
as I walk through life
setting a full table
for the ones I love
smiling talking hugging
the ones I love
shaping my words for
yes the ones I love

and yet there are
a thousand other shouts
turning heads and
begging for adoration and
fragmenting attention
so I begin to wonder
how long I'll be

invisible

I suppose I don't want
always attention and
forever adoration and
endless thanks because

the pressure then
the expectations
would they not make
a person crumble

so perhaps it is better
to wear the name

invisible

though words go unread
and deeds go unnoticed
and love wears a cloak
that one cannot see
perhaps it is nobler
perhaps it is wiser

the problem is
the line between

invisible

and no longer here
is thin and blurry
and ever shifting
and I no longer know
which describes me

so please
won't someone
see hear feel me
just this once
so that I may know
I am not already
dead and gone
I am merely

invisible

The Beast

At times I am
a shimmering sea
of calm and collected,
and not a rock or a word
or even a kid whining
about the dinner to which
I've given the last hour
of my time can shake me
from that place.
I am the glass
reflecting a brilliant sun,
refusing to be pulled
into the winds around me.
I reflect the beauty in humanity.

And then, at other times,
I am a raging wave,
a hurricane sea,
with crests that swell
to insurmountable heights
and crush all that
stands in my way.
I cannot be contained,
I cannot be tamed,
I cannot be moved.

I reflect the beast in humanity.

The beauty and the beast
live in equal measure
within me, and there is
no knowing which it will be
at any moment in time,
except that it becomes
quite predictable when
one considers the patterns.

The beast
waits for me
in the kitchen.

My Mother

My mother did
the best she could.
Her best was enough—
she raised three kids
on her own, in all ways,
physical, financial, emotional.

It wasn't easy, but she
almost made it look easy—
almost, except for the days
we'd find her bent over bills,
wiping away tears she
didn't want us to see,

because she never wanted us
to know how bad things were.
She protected us from
the realities of her world,
even though the realities
of her world—our world—

leached into our knowing.
A father who left
so completely could not
be hidden forever.

She attended every
special ceremony, every
sporting event she could manage,
every teacher conference,
though she worked two jobs
for years of our lives.

Her presence gave us
the courage to try,
to become,
to walk into unknown lands
with our backs straight
and our chins up.

She couldn't spend whole days
chaperoning field trips or
a weekend attending my
senior trip with me, but
she was there in all the
ways that mattered.

Now I have children of my own.
I attend what assemblies I can,
the sporting events I can manage,
every teacher conference.

And on the days
I have to miss a field trip
or I can't attend an event
or I feel like I'm the worst mother
in the history of the world,
I remember:

The greatest lesson
my mother taught me
was that my best
as a mother
was good enough.

Rise

I want to
rise above.

It's hard though, see,
because so much of everything
depends on mindset,
what lives in the mind,
and what lives in my mind
is belts and words like whips
and not good enough and
all the empty spaces—
how does one rise above
a past that feels so heavy
and crooked and
enormous?

We got a call today that said
a camp my sons and I
were eagerly awaiting
had been canceled, and
we've all been at each other's throats
for months now, counting down
the days until we're saved
by Family Camp, and now,
because of ten inches of rain,

even that hope has been
taken from us, and
all I can think
       all I can think
              all I can think
is that we'll never get to
do something like this on our own,
we'll never have the money
to experience the freedom of a family retreat,
we'll probably never be able
to give them a fun vacation
during the summer,
because it's so damn hard
to rise above that impoverished past,
and sometimes I get weary
of trying.

Their daddy says we should
just pack everybody up and
go to the neighborhood pool,
let off some steam, swim away
a little disappointment.
So we do, and they all swim
while I sit in a chair brooding
because maybe I'm not ready
to get in a swimsuit yet.
I watch them, and the sun

catches just right on the water,
making it shimmer and sparkle
in the exact place where
my sons congregate,
and I'm momentarily blinded.
They move away and I can
see them more clearly and the
sky turns a bit bluer and
the wind a bit gentler and
the trees a bit taller and
I feel the strength move all the way
through me, rousing hope:
maybe I *can* rise above
maybe I can rise
maybe I can—

I want to
rise above.

My Father

He drove with
no real purpose in mind
I think he just liked driving
liked how it felt
to leave anywhere and
not know if he would
ever return

Real Courage

i

I'm not always kind to them. In fact, I have to yell a lot to get their attention, and every time I do it, I feel bad, guilty, despicable, even, but what do you do when so many people are talking at the same time?

ii

I'm not always happy, either, because this is hard work, and it feels so isolating living consumed by endless needs and not having the space or breathing room or time to sit down and have a quick meal with adult friends. How does anyone maintain friendships when kids suck the social marrow from your bones? It is not a happy surrender. It's not that I miss my old life, exactly. I know—I remember how—in that former life, I always longed for something different, something better. It's just that kids are hard. They require constant energy and give zero breaks—a twenty-four-hours-a-day full-time job with no vacation time. I knew what it would require, but who does, completely?

iii

I'm not always a good mother. I don't pay attention like I should, don't always watch them play or sit to join them, because I'm so tired—so tired—and sometimes I'm afraid

I'll regret all this time I spend doing other things (there are always other things) when they're grown and gone and no longer living under the roof of my home, the roof of my love. Will I regret my work? Will I wish I had played with them more, observed them more? Sat still more? Sometimes these questions keep me awake at night. Sometimes I don't like their answers. Sometimes I promise to do better and then a new day begins and the old habits swallow me.

iv

Sometimes I wish I could be different or they could be different or something, anything about this situation, could be different, but wishes aren't as easy to believe in, since I'm not a six-year-old girl anymore, and you know what? Motherhood wasn't meant to be easy, it was meant to shape me and remake me and put me back together whole. Becoming something greater isn't ever easy or simple.

v

My great-grandmother once told me that real courage is knowing you're beat before you begin and then doing it all anyway. She stole the words from someone else, but what she meant could be boiled down to what every mother knows: Real courage? Motherhood.

Growing

There is a rock,
not enormous, not impassable,
but large enough to make
the traveler stop, turn back,
look at his mother,
who watches from the wings.
He is uncertain:
Should he climb?
Should he circumvent?
Should he trace his steps
back to safety and warmth and love
because this rock is unknown
and he is still learning
strength?

It is the face of his mother
that urges him on.
It is her eyes,
squinting to see
the rock that, perhaps,
does not look so large
from where she watches.
It is her smile as she looks
at him, her gentle nod
that speaks words he

cannot hear but can feel,
instead, in the middle
of his chest.
Go on, it says.
You can do hard things.

And so he does.
He climbs the rock.
He reaches the other side,
and when he looks back again,
the rock disappears,
fades clean away.

And he is bigger.
Stronger.
Wiser.

His mother waves.
He lifts his hand and
moves on his way.

Nature's Greatest Creations

one bids you goodbye
at the door of a car

and before pulling out
you stare at the window

where the two do not sleep
but simply wait for you to leave

so they can take their
wild out of hiding

your eyes fall to the door
where you left three of them

making blanket forts
but actually making

nothing more
than a mess

and then you drive
and you wish you could be

driving anywhere

but you are bound by time

and a doctor waiting in
a room with crinkly paper

you have a heart-to-heart chat
and four times she asks you

if you want some
extra protection

and five times
you say no

because though there are
six of them spread around the table

and though there is a seventh
claiming space in your heart

but not here
with you

though you would die
or maybe simply go a little crazy

if there were eight

you think that doing it

the natural way is really
the best way

nature knew what
it was doing, right

and all you have to do
is look at nature's way

to understand what happened
and the wonder of it all

yes the wonder of it all—
it is a wonder—

and maybe you want to
hold on to the wonder

she leaves nine minutes
after she walks into your room

and catches you on the way out
where you talk for another few minutes

laughing about the stories

you could tell with that full house

and then you drive the
ten minutes home

where some of nature's
greatest creations

live

Absurdity

Some would call
my life impossible.

They look at the
cramped nature of it,
the absurd imagining of it,
the cracks in a veneer
that's touted as the
end of all ends,

                the great American dream.

I look at my life and see
the roadblocks that bar me
from entering unknown pathways,
a former life that, if I were
inclined to analyzing,
would tell me I could be
nothing more than this.
I see the implausibility
of plans and dreams that
wave steady in a heart
patched together with
puckering scars.

It is impossible
on the bad days.

But on the good days,
I find my eyes drawn
to a wide, expansive blue sky—
impossible, too—and my mind
seizes those moments of
overwhelming beauty,
those moments that make me
feel small in a way that
also makes me feel large,
those moments when the
whole world curls open to me.

I know that
one cannot ever attain
         the impossible

without first
attempting
         the absurd.

So I walk back to my
impossible, absurd life,

and I give it my best.

The Spaces

What we don't say
when you are here is that

I have so many
and you have none

that you think you could
do it better than I can

that maybe you should have
had them instead of me

that you are angry yours
did not live

that you are devastated yours
did not live

that you lost another
a week before you came

that you wish it could have
turned out differently

that you wonder if

it was your fault

that I have more
than I can handle

that you have
not enough

that what I have subtracts
from what you have

that your dream doesn't stand
much chance of coming true now

that life isn't
the least bit fair

that death
destroys us

that life goes on even when
we wish it would end

that you're thinking
of leaving

What we don't say

when you are here is

everything will be
okay

Life promises
nothing

With Joy and Gladness

there are times / when I long for / a completely different life / maybe only one kid / a friend sat on her porch / with her sister / talked about / the simplicity of the moment / the aching within me / was tangible enough / to feel a deep pinch / like something gripped my soul / kept it smaller / I would like to feel simplicity / I would like to be able / to sit on my back deck / for any moment / be glad for what I have / why can't I be glad / a friend told me / she would give anything / for what I have / she's been trying for years to have children / but it's easy to see / what's on the surface / harder to see what we don't know / I guess the same / can be true / on the other side of the equation / maybe a friend's simplicity / means kissing one child goodnight / yelling at her husband / going to bed alone / maybe you never really know / the truth of another's life / only your own / sometimes I wish / I could get out of my own head / I wonder if I would be glad then

To Be Lonely

what is worse

than feeling forgotten
    than believing we are invisible
than carrying the weight of loneliness

one who is forgotten is
    one who has lost importance
or perhaps never had it in the first place

a life lived forgotten

is not a life that generates waves
    is not a life that makes a difference
is not a life that lives

so the ones who are forgotten
    stumble through their lonely days
not knowing

whether they matter

where they have impact
    who might be watching
if anyone at all is watching

what is worse than feeling forgotten
      perhaps there are many things worse
but for those who feel forgotten

there is nothing

The Christmas Card

a check came in the mail
along with some money
to buy our kids Christmas gifts
from the grandparents they hardly know,
the card signed by the same sloping hand
I remember from sporadic cards
when I was a kid

the handwriting I always thought of
as cramped yet neat,
arranged in all capitals
like he'd never learned
the lowercase counterparts,
was nowhere near the *love you*
or *miss you* or *Merry Christmas*

so we have no record of his handwriting
so we see no evidence of his remembrance
so we begin to wonder if he
ever touched the greeting at all
as if the space of his world
could not be disrupted by
a single thought of us, come Christmastime

Good and Bad

i

it comes out / at the worst of times / swinging seething breaking / that twisted thing in me / sometimes it lies in wait / preparing itself / sometimes it comes / unbidden / but it leaves / the same fire in its stead / I try / I really do / I know all the tools / I have practice / I walk straighter / than I did / all those years ago / but this is me / a little good / a little bad

ii
tell me about your day, I said
I was a little good and a little bad, he said

we laughed at the honesty of it

but in what he said lies a deeper truth
one we don't always recognize

but instead try to justify away

I didn't know, we say
I didn't mean, we say

I didn't think it through, we say

it's not so terrible, is it
the simplicity behind everything we do?

there are two people down deep

dueling the days away
which one wins today?

iii
if you love me you must love
all of me

every part
every whole

every hold, too

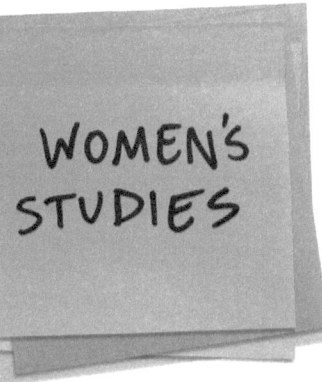

I Am a Woman

I am a woman.

I did not come into this world with a silver spoon in my pocket that told me every word out of my mouth was gold; I came into it with a fork in my side that said, *Stay quiet, stay invisible, stay obedient, because you and your kind have nothing of value to add.*

I am a woman.

I did not come into adolescence with a solid path laid out before me, straight and relatively unhindered; I came with a twisting path, a shifting path, a drop-out-from-beneath-my-feet path that said the only way I could be somebody was if I was this size, if I had this hair, if I shaved my legs, if I folded myself inside this box, if I didn't argue, if I passively watched my world unroll before me rather than grabbing it with both hands.

I am a woman.

I did not come into adulthood with an eye already fixed on the prize assured me; I came with an eye assessing the steep climb that would lead to maybe more value and maybe fairer pay and maybe a better chance to prove that I do have something important to contribute.

I am a woman.

I did not come into the world with anything promised me except that others have bravely worn this title of woman and have even so shifted the trajectory of the world.

I am a woman.

She Said Something

She said something,
she pointed fingers,
she raised the alarm
on a fault line that shifts
beneath the surface of things
but never quite bubbles out
from beneath the cement slab of
fame, fortune, politics.

She said something,
she pointed fingers,
she raised the alarm—
but, in the end,
she was a woman.
Easily dismissed as
hysterical,
melancholic,
female.

This is the Story of a Girl

i

be beautiful, but don't cross the line to sexy: you never know what kind of trouble that will bring

work as hard as a man—and then some—if you want the same wage (you still won't get it), and also give everything you have to your kids and partner: if you don't, you're not a real woman

make it all look easy: if it's not you're probably doing something wrong

be brave: don't let them push you around, but also don't stand up for yourself too often or you might be called an abomination, a bully, a ball-busting bitch

make sure you have kids: but not too many or they'll call you a whore, tell you to keep your legs closed since you're the only one responsible for all those kids, and shame you for not having an abortion while in the next breath condemning abortion

be your own person: but take care you don't speak or write or act passionately about issues that concern you, lest you be called an aggressive feminist—their version of an insult

don't let them get away with sexual harassment or assault: but if you blow the whistle you'll be ruined

your body belongs to you: but it could also belong to him —and him—and him

know who you are but make sure you walk the line and stay in your place

ii
or you could just burn it all down

This is the Story of a Woman

I wear thin skin.
I cry easily.
I am often discounted.

I don't run in my very safe neighborhood after dark alone.
I don't walk down sketchy streets alone.
I don't wander into new and novel places alone.

I have been owned.
I have been made to feel small.
I have had my power stolen from me.

I have been catcalled, propositioned, inappropriately touched, pressured to do what I didn't want to do, cornered.

I have known the shame of insignificance.
I have known fear.
I have known the absence of security.

My body belongs to me.
My mind belongs to me.
My power belongs to me.

I am strong.

I am courageous.
I am worthy.

I am as intelligent as any man.
I am as innovative as any man.
I am as persistent as any man.

I am every woman.

Judgment

They can rape you
and get away with it.
They can fondle you
and get away with it.
They can say things
that make you uncomfortable
and get away with it.

It doesn't matter
that you're entitled
to due process or retribution
or, at the very least,
protection from rape or
unwanted fondling or
insensitive comments.
They don't even know
what justice means anymore.
Judgment is made before
the first witness is called—
upon first sight, really.
They only need a good, long look
to see you for what you are:
a girl who doesn't know
the difference between
sexual harassment and

an appreciation
of beauty.

Silly little girl.

Things They Told Me As a Teenager

If you walk out the door like that,
you're asking for trouble.
Men aren't responsible for their lust;
it's just the way they are.
You shouldn't dress that way.

I know why it happened.
Look what you're wearing.
Did you have a few drinks, too?
You probably wanted it.
This is your fault.

If you tell, they won't believe you.
That's the nature of life.
A man's word is truer than a woman's word.
Seal your mouth with the plug of patriarchy.
And get used to it, dear.

Besides, you liked it.

Here is My World

stay small, they said,
all those voices rising
from a distant past—
it could be mine or simply
the past of all those like me

you are a woman, they said
we are not comfortable
with your contrarian opinion
which is just another way of saying
shut up

you have nothing
valuable to contribute
to this conversation, they said
when I opened my mouth
to disagree—

because I feel too much
because I am sensitive
because I am taking things
the wrong way

because I am offensive

let it be
stay in your place
smooth down the waves

we learn early from those
who look on us to agree
with their every brilliant statement—

disgusting or clean
educated or ignorant
critical thinker or rote repeater

I humanize the world for them
give them a person instead of a vague idea
and they turn away
roll their eyes

she's just another silly woman, they say

A Secret

I move without anyone noticing,
without ears tuned to my voice,
without eyes fixed on my efforts,
without mouths cheering me on or
sounding an alarm

but the thing
about invisible is
they never
see you coming

Things They Said to Me

Stop complaining, I don't want to hear it.
Don't be like her, crying over every little thing.
You sure did get bigger since last summer, and by bigger I mean…
Worrying never added a day to anybody's life, but it sure does steal one.
What were you thinking?
License and registration, ma'am—hey, you're going to senior prom with my nephew. I'll let you off with a warning.
Life never came with any handouts.
You can be anything you want to be if you put your mind to it.
Well, kids, shit happens.
Your daddy never cared about anyone in his life. That's men for you.
Show your work.
You gotta do what they tell you first and then you can break the rules.
Call me when you get home.
Run away with me and get married.
Here's your ring.
You have the Patton forehead: big, shiny, proud.
Now, I don't want to hear that sniveling.
Eat. You'll waste away.

I bought you something at Long John Silver's. You're looking a little too thin.

You're gonna marry that boy someday.

It's like you have the golden touch.

You're too hard on yourself. No one's perfect.

Things will be all right. You'll see.

Don't be so silly.

You want to hang it all out where they can see it?

I'm sorry I was late.

You don't ever call anyone a name like that. I don't care what they've done.

No, you can't go see your boyfriend.

I don't have time for this. Go get lost in a book or play outside. You look like you could use some sun.

You sure are smart.

Roll, dammit. Don't just fall, roll.

Maybe you could help me study in my dorm room.

How would you like to be from a family with money?

And then there's you.

Watch your step. Can't be too careful on ice.

I'm afraid I'll have to ask you to leave. You're not allowed to do that now.

Don't you ever have any fun?

You're so uptight. Shake it out a little.

You have how many kids?

It goes by so fast. Enjoy it while you can.

Couples need to know they're sexually compatible before

they get married, don't you think?

Tie your shoes. Don't want you to trip over them.

I'd like to see you try.

Get me some milk.

I want to play outside, but I can't find my shoes.

I need you to help me fix my bike.

Always pay the closest attention to names. They're the most important part, and if you spell it wrong, you've just discredited yourself.

Lay off the clutch, we're rolling backward. Lay off the clutch. LAY OFF THE CLUTCH!

Five horses. Right now, at the whistle blow.

I just want everyone to know you're not perfect.

If you ever cross the finish line looking like a beauty queen, I swear to God…

Don't be nervous. It's just a little friendly competition.

Who do you think you are?

The Red Umbrella

Beneath a red umbrella,
she walks the
streets of her city,
clad in black,
the color of mourning.
She's not mourning,
she's unfolding.
There has been a death, yes,
but the grief of it
is not oppressive.
It is deliverance.

The wind blows.
She closes her eyes.

Surprises

I have never enjoyed surprises.

For one they disrupt my routine
and if there was ever a person

to thrive on routine it is me

While a nice surprise might be
welcome to other people, to me

a surprise is disturbing, as though

an entire world has
fallen apart and I don't know

which way to turn or look or step

because there is
no ground

beneath me

so this makes the surprises of life
hard to bear, of course

I used to struggle against them

used to go over and over and over
in my mind what I would possibly do if…

and then the first surprise hit me,

and it really wasn't so bad,
made life a little more interesting,

sharpened me,

and while I can't say, exactly
that I have come to welcome

the surprises of life

I have, at least
come to appreciate them—

at least when they are few and far between.

The Stages of Womanhood

You are three when you believe *I'll be back soon* means tomorrow.
You are five when you believe soon must mean different things to different people.
You are seven when you believe the world is mostly a safe place.
You are eight when you believe it's not at all—in fact, it's exceedingly unsafe. Cruel. Terrifying.
You are nine when you believe love is freely given, makes no conditions, and lasts forever.
You are eleven when you believe love has to be earned, it makes conditions, and it only lasts as long as you can measure up.
You are twelve when you believe skinny equals beautiful and beautiful equals good enough.
You are thirteen when you believe something you might do could bring him back.
You are fifteen when you believe he's not coming back—probably because of you.
You are sixteen when you believe the world is still yours to conquer.
You are seventeen when you believe maybe the world isn't actually yours to conquer—but you are definitely the world's to conquer.
You are eighteen when you believe that not eating at all

while running six miles a day will make you skinny, which makes you beautiful, which makes you good enough.

You are twenty when you believe you'll be alone all the rest of your days, because who could possibly love you?

You are twenty-one when you believe you could never be happier—you've found a partner who loves you for you, imperfections and all.

You'll be twenty-five when you believe life could not possibly get any better.

You'll be twenty-nine when you believe life could not possibly get any worse.

You'll be thirty when you believe the person in the mirror needs a change—maybe just a haircut, maybe a whole new body (yes, that's probably it).

You'll be thirty-three when you start to believe that maybe you're kind of a little bit beautiful after all.

Roar

They are outside screeching on the trampoline. All day they have been at each other's throats, uncooperative, uncommunicative, unloving, but now they are in bright sunshine and cool breeze and under a wide, soft blue sky, and they have summoned a vestige of peace. I feel unrest, though. Their voices clang into me, screeches of joy, shouts of direction, collections of giggles. They are the next generation, and what is this world in which they find themselves? A world in which a woman must apologize for her rape, her harassment, her discrimination because it damages the reputation of a man; a world in which a woman is viewed as an object to be desired, owned, manhandled, subjugated in every despicable way; a world in which a man can excuse himself from the responsibility of respect and honor of another gender with a laugh, a hand gesture, and a brow-raised look at the locker room. This is not the world I want for them. Their laughter twitching in through the cracks of my back door is innocent and pure, and this is how I want them to remain. One will turn ten this month, and on the way into the library recently, he told me he thinks he might like a girl; he's not entirely sure, because feelings are confusing. I told him he can like a girl if he wants, because, for now, it's somewhat harmless—but what will my sons learn from the world? What will they see? What will they do? No matter how I fail as a parent, a mother, a woman, they will never see Woman as an object to be dismissed, cast aside, devalued. I will roar it in my home until it roars into their hearts: Woman matters.

Woman

She stood before him,
yellow skirt flipping
around her childish legs
in a wind that bent the tree
where she had once seen
two snakes fall from the sky
and then watched her mother slay them.
He kicked a leg over the side
of his motorcycle,
said I'll be back,
see you later,
don't cry for me.
But when will you come back? she said.
Tears carved her cheeks.
He smiled and drove away
and she never got her answer.

She stood before him
the summer she turned twelve
only a girl still,
and the ache of home,
the ache of familiarity,
followed her through an unknown house.
So she cried herself to sleep
and he heard what her tears

spoke without words.
Don't be like her, he said.
Too soft and sensitive and melodramatic.
It's easy enough, isn't it?
But do you love me? she said
Fear squeezed her heart.
He smiled and sent her back home
and she never got her answer.

She stood before him
with a man and a boy at her side,
not much a girl anymore,
and the blue tarps stretched
over roofs were nothing compared
to the tarp around her heart,
covering the wind-blown places
and all the missing shingles.
I'm sorry, he said.
I never meant to hurt you.
I've always loved you.
Yes, she said, but did you want me?
Was I enough?
Am I beautiful?
He smiled and let her go
and she never got her answer.

Yet the unanswered

shaped her into a
woman.

The South

I labored
over the way
I spoke.

I knew you could tell a lot
about a person by
the way she spoke.
I liked using large words
that told a story of education
and refinement. I liked
turning thoughts over
in my mind, shaping them,
then letting them loose.
I liked offering the truth.

And yet the drawl
seemed to be a
disqualification
of some kind.

So I listened to the people
around me who had the
southern sound that made them
appear a bit slow, a bit naive,
a bit empty of important ideas,

I took note of the problem areas,
excavated them all,
surgically removed
the southern from my speech,
because I wanted to be more
than that corner of the world.

I took pride in their
astonishment that I was
from Texas, that I had lived
in the state all my life and had
managed to escape
that distinct way of speaking,
the peculiar drawn-out vowels,
the meandering curvature
of language.

But the south does not
only live in the words
that flow from mouths.
There were other ways
my southern roots would
creep out, and eventually
I would be fine with the
visible clues of my heritage,
because the south boasts
its own victories:

charm, manners, compassion.

Generations

1

She loved him first and last, until the day he died and long after. She continued loving him in her steady, unbroken way, though it meant spending more than forty years alone, though it meant living the rest of her days in a falling-apart house he'd built in the middle of a neighborhood that turned dark around her, that fell from the heights it was named for. She was known as the little old lady with white hair who would walk the streets greeting people by name. None of her neighbors knew that she slept with a pistol under her pillow, just in case, but she was a legend among all her great-great grandchildren.

2

Her daughter loved a music man who beat her on the worst days and wrote her songs on the best. They met in a dance hall. He played guitar, she played a wicked fiddle. Her mama and daddy didn't much approve of him, because they were Southern Baptists and didn't believe in dancing, but she married him anyway. He drank too much, touched too hard, yelled too loudly, but she loved him all the way through the living of a daughter and the dying of a son who drove too fast around a slippery curve, too much like his daddy, and she loved him even after he dropped down dead in the middle of the garden she always thought he loved more than her.

3

Her daughter loved a man who found another right after she'd given him a long-awaited son. She'd made some mistakes, a whole twenty years of them, but she believed he'd made the biggest one—leaving. She could never forgive him for that. But forgiveness isn't required for love, and she never married again, loving him until the day she took a fall inside her lonely house and punctured her stomach on the edge of a table and bled herself dry in all the internal places while lying on a table in an incompetent intensive care unit. They revived her, but only partially, her brain left too long without oxygen. What else was there to live for, anyway? The gaping loneliness? She'd rather not.

4

Her daughter married a man who was handsome, charming, and reckless, who sang in her ear on the day he spun her round the wedding dance floor, she in her white puffy sleeves, he in his bright white tuxedo, two figures from the pages of a 1970s magazine. She thought she'd found love, because hers unfolded like a novel, but his, well, it was more like a short story, or a series of them, and after a time she realized they were writing two different tales in two different genres and it was time to give up, leave, try again. And that's exactly what she did, and she found love in another, and this love was a novella, not quite as long as it might have been, because they did not begin as early as they might have, but they are still loving, today, in a house that sits above the ground, safe and warm and quiet, with windows she can open for the first time in her life.

5

I am her daughter. I married a man who is strong and kind and loyal. My love is more like an epic novel, like *War and Peace*, bursting with pages and battles and peaceful resolutions so I have come to understand it as something entirely other-worldly, something that shimmers in the corners of a life, something that shapes us more than we could hope to shape it. Love that stands the test of time becomes, gradually, a classic tale to be enjoyed again and again, made greater and truer and more profound for all its detours traversed by the generations that carried it before.

The Woods, the House, and the Weather

Every now and then
I take a walk in those
woods of my memory,
pine needles bending
beneath my feet,
cicadas humming,
leaning trees towering up to the sky,
looking much taller than
they ever did
when I was grown.

The woods made room
for a house with a glass square
cut out of its ceiling,
where we could see, upon waking,
what sort of weather
waited for us outside.
We could never predict
the sort of weather waiting for us
in the next room, though.
Some days it was gray and foggy
and no one said a word, only let
the unspoken boil at the
edges of awareness.
Some days met a freezing rain,

contempt dripping from the ceiling
and wrapping around our ankles
so we could only stand there in its blast,
our bodies growing mercifully numb enough
so nothing seemed to hurt anymore.
Some days shone yellow and promising,
but those were the worst sorts of days,
deceptive with their golden smile,
the sorts of days that lived only in dreams
that would, inevitably, give way
to the sorts of days that exist
only in nightmares.
In a matter of minutes,
the sunny, cheery weather
could turn and rip us from
calm to hurricane, where we'd all
twist and turn around words and
accusations and expectations that felt
too far from our grasp, always, forever.

Those days all ended
the same way, though,
because he loved that old
rocking chair out front.
He'd sit, a cigarette glowing
between his thumb and first finger,
blowing rings of smoke

out into the woods,
up into the trees.

As if he hadn't just blown
the whole house
into oblivion.

The Photograph

The photograph sits in an
old plastic bin.
In it you are smiling,
as you were always smiling,
with a light that welcomed the world
and turned it lovelier.
In it you are young,
as you always appeared to be,
though you would grow older
and lose some of your hair and
make decisions that would
spin wheels on the shoulders of streets.

It was a birthday party, I think.
We were just kids,
lining beans on a butter knife,
trying to see who could balance
them all the way to the finish line
at the end of the sidewalk.
We were just kids
playing Red Rover,
twisting on a tire swing,
doing cartwheels under magnolias.
We were just kids
eating chocolate birthday cake

and triangle-cut sandwiches.

We were just kids.

We couldn't wait to grow up.
But it was the growing up
that would take you.
It was the falling in love,
the falling out of love,
the fighting, the making up,
the fighting again.
It was the walking away,
the believing you were invincible,
the carelessness of a danger
you never saw coming.

They could not keep you.
We could not keep you.
But, even so, you are here
preserved in a photograph
of a smiling boy
and a birthday girl
who knew nothing of the world
but looked on the future
with great expectation.
The sun shines in that photograph.
The sky beams blue,

and there is no hint
of what would come,
no knowing what life promised us,
nothing that we could not do.

You stare at the camera.
I stare at you, as if, even then,
I knew you were not
meant to stay.
And though time would take you,
it would not have you then,
for a moment in time,
a moment of memory
when you played
and watched and sang
and raced and spun and
lived.

In a fading photograph,
you live forever—
forever laughing, forever loving,
forever breathing, forever smiling
a boyish grin that reaches
between the fingers of time
into the space of the living.
This photograph is all that's left
to remind me you

ever lived at all.

Historical Examination

You sort through your history—

this one died from complications
after running into a door,
this one from a rabid squirrel bite,
this one from a lung disease,

they were all unlucky people,
weren't they?

Their daddy was a
railroad conductor,
which sounds so romantic

here are all their birthdates
and old-fashioned names
and death dates written
on a slip of paper:

Hattie and Viola and
Howard and James,

one was a writer, one was a poet,
another laid railroad tracks
in every sort of weather

you can trace them all back,
on down the line, roots from
Spain and France and settlements
in New York but mostly Texas

you squint at the fine print,
pore over the pages,

try to find what's left of them all
and at the end of the
searching and studying—

you still don't have any idea who you are

Hey There, Brother

Hey, there, brother—
come sit with me
beneath the moon
and its silver trees
and we'll talk about
the days of old—
the days before life
grew heavy and stole

what happiness we had left

Tell me, brother—
do you remember
the field where we
would run together
straight to a place
we'd disappear—
where safe wore bones,
where we couldn't hear

the angry words he said?

Let's think about
the tree out back,
the tire swing

all shining black
and in the heights
a fort to climb
for imagining
a better time

where pain could not break us

Come walk with me
through faded past
and wonder years
that could not last
suppose we find
a shred of hope
in days gone by
a valley's slope

suppose they can remind us

suppose…

We listen to what
our younger years say
of survival and love
and living and brave

and we make it out of this.

Hey there, brother—
come sit with me
and time will tell
our history

and history will tell the truth.

First Lines of a Female's Years

1. Where are you going, little brown mouse? Period.
2. It was the best of times. Period.
3. Little girls shouldn't argue. Period.
4. Families have their own trials. Period.
5. Crying makes you weak. Period.
6. A screaming this way comes. Period.
7. A beating also this way comes. Period.
8. You better not tell. Period.
9. You'll never be a writer. Period.
10. Don't be like her. Period.
11. It was the worst of times. Period.
12. Your lips look like you're wearing a constant pout. Take off your bitch face. Period.
13. Skinny equals beautiful. Period.
14. Your nose is too pointy. Period.
15a. Sexual purity is your mandate. No man wants damaged goods for a wife. Period.
15b. And you exist to become a wife. And a mother. Period.
16 a. I met him not long after my life split up. Period.
16b. One morning I found myself transformed into a monster. Period.
17. My father was dead to begin with. Period.
18. You go to college to get married, not educated. Period.
19. Everybody has their own mess. Period.

20a. If you don't first succeed, try harder. Period.

20b. But make sure you stay in this box made for you. Period.

21. My father gave me some advice that I've been eradicating from my mind ever since. Period.

22. I was to remember that afternoon my father took me to discover fire. Period.

23a. This isn't a place for a woman. Period.

23b. You are nothing but a woman. Period.

23c. You will never be anything but a woman. Period.

24. All that happens is how we interpret it, but know this: the world is not made for you. Period.

25. I don't feel like getting into it, if you want to know the whole lie of it. Period.

26. It was hate at first sight. Period.

27. Call me whatever you like. Period.

28a. For a long time, I never went to bed. Period.

28b. Do you know what they do to women who speak? Period.

29. I will buy the flowers myself. Period.

30. I am invisible. Period.

31. It was a pleasure to burn bridges. Period.

32. Someone died today, or maybe yesterday. Period.

33. I will torch the place in the blaze of my awakening. Period.

Memory

I used to have all the phone numbers of my friends memorized. It took too much time and effort to bend over and get the address book my mother kept on a small table where our rotary phone sat. Adona, Rachael, Sarah, Barbara, I could dial them all as soon as I decided to call them, and I knew the touch of the spinning dial and how long it would take to key in the numbers. I knew their addresses and their birthdays and what they loved to do after school and how many brothers and sisters they had and whether they had a dad.

These days I keep phone numbers in a digital log on my phone. All I have to do is remember names. I pull up the name, and the number already stares at me from the glow of my screen. Sometimes, in the ultimate automation, I tell my phone who I'd like to call, and my phone does all the work for me.

My memory needs to do nothing.

But the birthdays remain. They are like a permanent calendar of events in my mind. September twenty-fifth, June nineteenth, June eleventh, August eighth, August fourth, January twenty-eighth, January third, March seventh, March ninth. All the people who were important to me at some time or another, lodged indefinitely into the days of my mind.

Fifteen Years Ago

We crash landed
that night

but I think of it still
with such pleasure it burns my chest

I made him turn out all the lights
he made me relax

it was over before it began
but it began before it was over

and has continued on and on
for these fifteen years

Way Back When

When you were a kid
you used to read in a hammock
strung between two oak trees
outside your house
because it was a means
of escape

When you were a kid
you threw a pecan
at your sister and blamed
the resulting lump on your
grandma's boyfriend

When you were a kid
you would explore the cornfields
that waved from across the street
dreaming of the treasures
that might be hidden inside—
maybe even a new dad
as impossible as that might be

When you were a kid
you watched *The Goonies*
and freaked out about
skeletons and dying—

because you knew that
someday death would
come for you, too

When you were a kid
you shared a room with
your sister and fought over
clothes, curling irons, and makeup

When you were a kid
you lay in your bed and
stared up at the ceiling
imagining that your dad
was on a trip and would
walk in any minute

When you were a kid
you wondered what was
wrong with you because
you thought kids were
what made parents leave

When you were a kid
you endured the endless
hours of a day and wondered
what to do with them
in a place that had

nothing to do

When you were a kid
you couldn't wait to get
out of there
and when you did
you missed it

Read

I started working
when I was fifteen,
in a greasy fast-food joint,
where the smell of oil
clung to my hair and
twisted my stomach at night.
I only lasted two weeks,
because I was better
than fast food,
and sure enough,
my next job was a
sandwich artist.
I lived up to that title,
artfully arranging
those sandwiches and
rolling them up good and tight.
I was the best sandwich artist
there ever was.

At eighteen, I moved up,
worked the late shift at a
convenience store,
four days a week, after school,
opening on Saturday mornings
when men would come in for beer

to take on their fishing expeditions
or some coffee to take on a road trip
or fifty bucks' worth of
scratch-off lottery tickets
they'd stand outside the doors
and rub off right in front of me.
When they didn't win,
they'd come back in with
another fifty-dollar bill,
slide it across the counter.

After that, the jobs came much easier—
news reporter, features reporter,
editor, managing editor,
and then, at thirty-three,
my first lay-off.
It felt like a sign.
I'd already worked hard
for nearly twenty years.
Now all I wanted to do
was read.

So I do.

Home

1
The house floated
it seemed
When the corn was growing

we'd play hide and seek
among its stalks
soon as they grew tall enough

The rest of the time
that field lay empty
with mud ruts

that twisted ankles
when we moved on to a
game of chase

but still we played
there was
nothing else to do

in a town
as small
as this one

2

I remember the day
I walked through
those barren ruts

stumbling forward
water waiting at the
end of them

and there was a
great black cloud of
blackbirds following me

like I had walked onto
the set of an
Alfred Hitchcock film

I raced home to safety
to security
to satisfaction

3

Snakes came out
every spring
looking for food

and I vowed

they would
not get me

kept my feet curled up
in the hammock
a book propped on my belly

4
I looked around that
falling-apart house the first time
I brought a friend home

I saw the holes in the porch
the door that stuck tight
the green stains all up

the white side of the house
caused by excessive humidity
and not enough time to clean it

I felt a flush of shame
walking in and out of the rooms
seeing through another's eyes

those dirty windows and
rust-colored carpet and
the ceiling I could touch

even before
I was all the way
grown

5
I hated it
because I had to
call it home

I hated it
because it was clear
to see that it was

not much of one
though my mother
tried

I hated it
because it told a
deeper story, as most things do

It said
Once poor
always poor

6
I made it my mission
to never be poor
to never again feel that shame

7
The home is gone today
torn down to make room
for another

and my someday
was torn down
with it

because watching
that home disappear
in the pictures my mother sent

was like watching a past life
fade into never-been
and I knew I couldn't let it go

So I held on to her pictures
and I studied the chipping paint
and I wondered how life

might have been different

without
that first home

It would not
have been better—
that I know for certain

Conclusion

No one ever talked to us
about the way things were.
No one really talked
about much of anything.

This was all we knew:

1. Sometimes our mother
would cry behind a closed door.

2. Sometimes our father
would join her
behind the closed door,
and we would hear
their raised voices
but not what they said.

3. Reduced lunches
in the school cafeteria.

4. Our mother
worked three jobs
then two.

5. "Your father

has another family."

6. "A girl who's three,
a boy just born."

7. "We're getting
a divorce."

8. He never called
but for the rare occasion
and never on our birthdays.

9. We were not
The Replacements.
We were
The Replaced.

10. Sometimes people
from church
brought us food.

11. There was a giant hole
in our front porch
the screen door was
put on the wrong way
the front door stuck
so tight sometimes we

couldn't get out or in
without help.

I was eleven years old
old enough to know things
but no one ever talked to us
about the way things were.

Any truth is
far better than
a child's conclusion.

Stories

What do I know
of my family's stories?
Not as much as I would
like to know. I have not
made the space to sit down
and listen to them.
I don't know all the stories
of my parents, and they
don't know all the stories of me.
We exist as two-dimensional
characters, where we might
become three- and four-dimensional.

It's important to know
the stories of where
you came from.

I must know that my father
once stopped at a red light,
took a baseball bat out of his car,
smashed the headlights
of another car, because
the driver cut him off in traffic;
it tells me I was not the only
recipient of his anger.

It's vital for me to know
that my mother loved her father
even though he left her,
because then I know how
to love mine.
It's imperative to know
the story of my great-grandfather,
who was rumored to have beaten
my great-grandmother
on the bad days and work
in his garden on the good ones
so that I can then understand
what it means to endure,
what it means to love the best
and not the worst,
what it means to be
knocked down to the bottom
of the world and
rise again.

Stories soften us in the places
we've stiffened and hardened.
They can crack across a landscape
of hurt and distrust and disappointment
and give us a sense of belonging—
because when you know
the stories of your family,

you know where you belong.
They tell us who we are and
who we might possibly become.
They are an inheritance,
a sparkling ocean that invites us
to walk upon them.
Colossal.
Enchanting.
Life-giving.

Stories show me
how to be human—
a walking contradiction
of myself.

Tapestry

The people in my formative years,
who sat in a classroom with me—

the girl whose breasts showed up
in third grade and made the
rest of us tell our mothers
we needed bras already—

the boy who danced
like Michael Jackson
in the gym and made
all the girls swoon—

the teachers who
whispered that
I might be more—

the peers who listened
when I spoke up, when I shook
through a speech on
graduation day—

the ones who stayed
all night in a gym and
played cards and won gifts

and wondered about our
collective futures—

the roommates who
lived with me so we
could afford rent—

the people I passed
and the ones who passed me
on that outdoor track
where I worked off
the cursed calories—

the ones who waited
in a school newspaper office—

the guy who welcomed
me to a new town,
my first newspaper job,
with his pants unbuttoned,
reaching for my arm though I
screamed and shook him off—

the man who took
a chance on me and
said yeah, sure, work here—

the reporters who
drew me into a family
that would make it hard
to leave—

the people who looked down
on anyone who made
as little as I did—

the ones who said
it couldn't be done—

the ones who didn't
pay attention until
I had something to give them—

the ones who said
I would never—

the ones who said
of course I would—

the man who told me
women could not work well
once they had children—

the woman who passed

my name along—

all the students who
sang my songs—

the couples I passed
on the streets holding hands—

the girls in red dresses
flanking an aisle—

the man I love—
the children I adore—
the dad who left—
the stepdad who filled in the hole—
the mom who believed—
the sisters and brothers who loved—

the aunts and uncles
and cousins and
grandparents—

they are all a part of me.

General Studies

Lessons

How many times
have I said yes
when I meant no?
I cannot count
them all.

Will you edit
this report for me?
Yes, of course.

If you loved me,
you would.
Yes, okay.

Quit your whining
and don't be like her.
Whatever you say.

Would you like a drink with that,
are you feeling okay,
will you be my planner,

will you take this story off my hands,
are you available to sing at my wedding,
should we have another baby,

do you want to go to this concert with me,
will you tell me what you really think,
do you still love me,

can you handle it,
can you hold this
for a minute (or a lifetime, maybe),

do you agree,
want to try this,
you want to actually

make some money
instead of being poor,
are you responsible,

are you crazy,
do you have a plan,
can you do it yourself,

do you know what
you did wrong,
do you want something to eat,

can you come,
will you do it,

can't you try harder?

Yes.
But no.
But yes, of course.

The greatest mistakes
I made in my life
happened when I said
        yes
where I wanted
to say
        no.

Real Courage

i
Real courage is knowing
you might be beat and trying
it anyway.

ii
Real courage is looking
into their doubting faces
and surprising.

iii
Real courage is going
against the grain and choosing
to swim upstream.

iv
Real courage is feeling
afraid and yet doing
what you must then do.

v
Real courage is being
who you are—unconcerned
with what they all think.

Afternoon Slump

What is it about
the afternoon slump?

The exhaustion
creeps over you
and all you want to do
is maybe doze off a little
in your chair while
no one is watching

except you know
your boss is kind of
an asshole and he'd probably
catch you and then
he'd likely fire you
for sleeping on the job—

he doesn't think a mother
can do anything outside
the home anyway—
and then you'd be
out of luck next time
the house bill came

they'd kick you out

you'd be homeless for the
first time in your adult life
you'd probably lose all your kids
who—let's face it—might be
better off without you by that point

and then you'd just be
another washed up
might-have been who
made the choice to
close her eyes and give in
to the afternoon slump.

That's the thing
about your luck—
you've never had any.

So, instead,
you make yourself
another pot of
tea.

Saving Seats

Save me a seat? she said.
He did. He waited
three whole hours,
watched the game without her.
She never showed.
By the end of it,
he understood the day
was a metaphor
for his life—saving seats,
yet sitting alone.
Saving seats was a
lonely man's
pursuit.

He left
and did not
look back.

Pretending

How many of us
walk around with our
silvery smiles and

shiny lives but
underneath is the
black shadow of

purposelessness
fear
hopes unfulfilled?

It's impossible to tell—
we've gotten so good
at pretending.

Compartments

Family
I don't always feel easy with the extended part, and the immediate one is exhausting, at least for now, but I love them all. They have made me, unmade me, remade me.

Work
I think about it all the time, carry my notecards around to record every little idea, every plot twist, every element that might be useful for later. It keeps me tethered to a moment and yet a million miles away.

Money
Not enough, never enough, what will we do, how will we do it, should we sell the house, I can eat less, will we make it, what if we don't, I wish, please.

Past
The regrets are piling up—if I had only handled that differently, if I hadn't done that, if I had chosen to go there, if I could turn back time, if I could do it all over again, if only.

Food
Don't look in the mirror, check the pooch, stay away from the scale, get on the scale, does this fit, do I even look

good, no I don't, I think maybe I'll skip dinner tonight.

Anxiety
The engine light's on, it could be anything, it's probably the worst thing, this is going to break us, how will we recover, we won't, we'll be out on the streets, this is how it ends

Hope
The feather flinches, shivers, throbs. It begins to beat once more.

Truth
One life, many compartments.

Wishes

I stood on a hill,
a dandelion in my hand.
The wind lifted
the first feathery petals
from the stem,
and for a moment,
they stared at me,
my wishes twirling
on air.

I released
the rest of them,
sent my white wishes
wherever it is
wishes go.

The Gathering Place

The rooms fill
with the shape of family,
some around the table,
some stretched out on the floor,
the hum of love
folding around them.

Memaw

They sold all her vintage
Agatha Christie books
to a secondhand bookstore.
They cleared out all her candy jars,
where she kept gummy orange slices
topped with granular sugar
and Riesen caramels
and an endless supply of Skittles.
They sold them in an estate sale,
where people who didn't know
their meaning or the way they could
mark a childhood with joy
and anticipation and comfort
bought them for ten cents.
They put her house on the market
and sold it in fourteen days.
They sold her old car, the one
with which she'd side-swiped mine
but about which I didn't have
the heart to tell her because
she was my grandmother,
so I drove it with a long,
straight scar marking
my driver's side door.

To me, they gave:
a glass trinket box
with a purple flower on it,
where I collect the rings
my sons buy me at their
holiday gift shop every year;
her old cake container
with her name, B. Dupree,
scrawled across the clear top
in permanent marker,
which I use to arrange
cupcakes for my sons'
birthday parties;
and her old china cabinet,
which stores all my sons' art supplies.
I think she would feel glad knowing
her things have moved on
to the next generation
and collect gifts,
fill bellies with sugary sweetness,
cultivate creativity.

But I sure would like
to have those old
Agatha Christie books
I always saw her reading,
her old candy jars

from which I pilfered
every chance I got,
her car that left its
paint on mine
or her home where we sat
watching the ten o'clock news.

Really, I would
simply like to have
her.

The Old

How do we leave the old, the familiar?

My husband asked me this today. Not these words, exactly. We were talking about a job he's had for the last year. Should he keep it? Money is tight, but it's added a bit more overwhelm to our schedule. It would give us a steady buffer, he says. Like it has been doing. But should he keep it?

I feel the tension—yes, we should keep it, no, it will slowly break us down if we do, and I find that I can settle on no real right answer. We are restless, but this is always how we get when we have been somewhere for a while—a flaw in our design, perhaps. Or is it simply that the horizon has grown familiar and we must break free of it before we can set our sights on a newer, better one?

My husband wakes the next morning and goes to work at the same place.

The old horizon has a magnetic pull.

In Another Life

In another life,

I might have been
the woman who walked in
wearing a dark pink shirt
and butterfly rings and
heels on her feet

with her carefully-kept hair
short around her face
and her makeup flawless
and two perfect little girls
trailing behind her.

I might have sat listening,
narrowing my mind a little
every time the speaker
opened his mouth.
I might have gone on

fancy dates with my husband
and not worried about the bill.
I might have sailed through college,
paid for by parents who had saved
for years to get me in and out,

I might have paid for
private lessons,
I might have learned
not to equate money with
the words *not enough*,

I might have approached
the end of the month
without a sinking feeling
that had been building
for days, weeks, months, years,

I might have looked at the sunrise
as a promise instead of another day
to fight for my place in the world,
I might have managed to rid myself
of this extra stomach flab,

since science tells us stress adds
pounds to our spare tire region,
I might have felt good enough,
noticed, important enough
to have something to say,

I might have been different,

or maybe not.

Every now and again,
a deep ache overtakes me
for the life I might have had
if not for the privation that
followed on my heels,

into every place,
all around.
It looked me in the eyes
at all turns,
in every face,

with every word.
It whispered what no child
should hear, and sometimes
I wish, for a moment or more,
that I could have lived that

other life, a wealthy life
with wealthy parents and
wealthy opportunities.
Maybe I could have
been better.

But mostly I am glad.

In my lack I built
my wings and learned
to fly them properly.
Bravely. Unapologetically.
I earned them,

scars and all.

Coffee: a Wondering

If a spoonful of sugar
makes the medicine
go down, then
what does a
spoonful of coffee do?

One sweet,
one bitter,
opposites—
if not completely,
then at least
marginally

Does coffee, then,
make the medicine
come up?

Collected Jokes that Aren't Funny

Why would you pay to subscribe to that worthless piece of paper?
I'm only kidding.

I had this coworker who was less—well, she was a real Butch character.
Lighten up—I'm just kidding.

He hasn't done a thing for our country since he was elected eight years ago—probably because he wasn't born here.
I'm just kidding.

Fat people are disgusting.
I'm kidding.

Journalists should be lynched for their misconstruction of the truth.
I'm just kidding.

Those millennials and their excuses. At a certain point you have to take responsibility for yourself, stop being slothful victims.
Really—I'm kidding.

Artists don't want a job; they're too lazy to work for someone else.
I'm kidding.

Women who have more than two kids are the least educated among us, just taking up space. No brains. Only child-bearing hips.
Wow. I'm kidding.

Black people are angry because they're making themselves look bad by doing what they've always done: lie, steal, cheat.
Seriously, I'm only kidding.

Black Lives Matter is stupid.
Hey—I'm just kidding.

A woman who's raped probably deserved it. (Like, have you see what she was wearing/how much she drank/how she acts?)
Geez! I'm kidding.

I'll tell you how I'd solve the drug cartel problem: put a bullet through the head of everyone who tries to cross the border illegally.
Whoa, now—I'm only kidding.

They said they had cracked pipes, not that they needed crack pipes. (So, no, Mr. President, don't send your druggie son, who has plenty of crack pipes, to help them. He's a worthless piece of addict shi—)
Oh my goodness, let's all be adults here—I'm just kidding.

Gay people don't deserve the same rights as me—God made Adam and Eve, not Adam and Steve.
Ha ha! I'm kidding.

Women don't deserve the same wage as men—they don't work as hard.
Can't you see I'm kidding?

Get in the kitchen where you belong, woman.
I'm just kidding.

There's no such thing as poor people—only lazy people.
I'm kidding.

There's this welfare guy who lives next to me and all he ever does is shout and complain and sit on his ass. Just like the rest of them.
I'm seriously kidding.

You look so good I could rape you.
Relax—I'm kidding.

A joke that devalues or dehumanizes another human being isn't a joke but a veiled atrocity, a forsaking of humanity, a vagrant violation of dignity and honor.
I'm kidding (or am I?)

Living

You want everything—

you want the shiny life,
the beautiful family,
the extravagant love,

the things, maybe,
the career, sure,
the dreams in a pocket,
waiting to take wing.

You want a bike you can
ride down the hill like
when you were a kid,
you want the past
without the kinks,

you want the nicer face,
the better figure,
the more fashionable clothes.

You want the circle of friends,
the lover who likes you,
the home to which you return
every night.

You want the time,
the energy, the sunrise
and the sunset but not
necessarily the nighttime
in between.

You want the stop time
and the go time
and the vacation time
and the fun time
and the fulfilling work time
and the truly loving time
and the take a walk time
and the meet with friends time
and the hang out with kids time
and the make love time
and the pursue dreams time
and you're a superstar time

and you want
them all in
equal measure.

You want it all,
but I'm telling you,
there has to be more

than having it all.

Well, there is, he said.
There is living.

PHILOSOPHY

The Truth About Small Living

We live small
because we are afraid—
afraid to fail at what it is
we have set our hearts upon,
so we put boxes around
our existence, trying
to keep ourselves safe.
We are unaware how, instead,
we keep ourselves
confined and restricted,
unable to stretch into our
full success and potential.

We are afraid of failing,
but mostly we are afraid
of succeeding, because
it would mean something—
it would propel us out upon
the precipice of the unknown,
it would demand we become
someone bigger than this
constrained version we are today.
We are afraid to take one step
into the field of dreams,
because it could mean

everything is different,
the stakes will rise,
we will never be the same.

We don't
really understand
that living small
is the same as
not living at all.

To College or Not to College

School was my savior, and
I mean that. Most of my friends
hated it, but for me it was
a way out, a way up
a way I could become
something better than I was
> *You don't need a college education*
> *anymore—you can be self-educated,*
> *spend all your time learning*
> *whatever you want to learn,*
> *studying only what's important,*
> *saving yourself whole years in the process*

See, not everyone has an easy
life, not everyone grows up
wealthy, not everyone has
the promise of education beyond
their borders, not everyone can see
another future beyond that of their parents
> *College is a giant waste*
> *of time and money*
> *no one should go to college*
> *talk about a terrible investment*
> *how's this one: four years,*
> *thirty-thousand dollars, working for someone else*

So maybe some don't need

the security of a degree
marking a wall, but that education
got me the hell out of dodge
It showed me I could really do this,
I could be someone, change my life, redeem my past

> *College can't do a thing for you*
> *that you can't do for yourself*
> *minus the debt, so just*
> *forget about it and do whatever*
> *you want, be whoever you want,*
> *start today, now, what are you waiting for*

Because the other thing is
not everyone believes they're
valuable, and you know what
growing up poor does to a person
Well, I do, honey, and it's
hard work breaking free of that iron-clad hold

> *What's the point of a degree*
> *you don't even use? I'm as skilled*
> *as others with business degrees,*
> *and I don't have the whopping debt*
> *hanging over my head*
> *I work for myself and make plenty of money at it, too*

Climbing out of that poor pit,
trying to be better and do better
when you watched your mom work
two jobs to put food on the table

while her own education dreams
vanished like your dad so you feel guilty about yours

> *Save yourself some time and*
> *mostly money, get to work*
> *today instead of wasting away*
> *in some class that won't move you*
> *a single inch along the scale of success*
> *You don't need college for some false legitimacy*

I'll tell you what education did
for me: It made me
Sure, I may not use my degree
anymore, but it offered me an escape
from my home, my past, my future
and I climbed somewhere that meant something for once

> *All you really have to do is focus*
> *It comes down to wanting it badly*
> *enough, you can always rise above*
> *your circumstances if you just*
> *try hard enough, you don't need*
> *college to lift you out of whatever pit you think you're in*

There are statistics that tell me what
I would have been without education
So I became instead a first-generation
college graduate, and I blazed, I shone,
I rose from the ashes and became me
That kind of education? You can't boil it down to a price tag

Here

What is happiness
but a forgetting of self,
a fading away of all circumstances,
a transcendence above
this moment in time—
this moment that exists
only now, only here,
only in the fullness
of a mind.

How is it that
past and future and
world and matter
all duel for their place
in my consciousness
when it is the here and now,
the time in which I am alive,
breathing in the smell of him
stretched out on a
gray blanket beside me,
that matters most?

This is the space,
the shape happiness takes:
a dim-lit moment when

all the rest fades away and
I reach for what often feels
out of reach.

I am forever chasing
the slippery hands of time,
willing it to speed,
willing it to slow,
but in this moment
time ceases to exist at all.

I pause,
it fades,
I breathe in the
dusty smell
of remembrance

here.

The One Right Way

Who are you to say
that the look on her face,
the one I know for joy
mixed with pride
mixed with pleasure
is one that comes
saddled with fear?

Who are you to say
that she who has worked
her entire life to get
where she is today,

(lived homeless,
lived desperate,
lived a life that appears,
at first glance, unfavored,
but is really, if one were to see
without the eyes of black and white,
just another hard-knock life,)

does not deserve
this simple pleasure,
this last opportunity
to make a home?

You cannot tell me
that the way she looks
when they all come piling
through her door

(because she has never had
anything like this,
not so nice, not so
beautiful, not so livable)

is not thoroughly
at peace with
this decision
she has made.

So you can call your shots,
say what's best,
try to convince
the world that
there is only one
right way in
every circumstance—

but who are you to say?

The Truth About Truth

The truth is adept
at going underground.

That's where it likes to hide out
because it prefers the dark.

We like our fake.

So we dig the hole
and bury our truth—

that we're barely holding on
that we're not making it

not even a little bit

that we can hardly pull ourselves
out of bed in the morning

because it's too windy and cold
and the world is weary and

we are weary

we wanted this and we got that

and now we don't really know

what to do with what we've
gotten except live a disappointing life

all the way to the finish

no it's not really disappointing
we're just frustrated because

our kid won't go to sleep
which means we can't go to sleep

which means tomorrow will be a nightmare

which means we'll probably
wake up in a bad mood

because have you seen us
on too little sleep?

We bury our truth

we lob it underground we fill
the hole so no one will even suspect.

But what does the truth

do underground?

It grows.

Unanswered

What do you think
you should do?

He always asked
the question after
some misdemeanor
or the coming of a crossroad

but he never
specifically told me
what I should do or
what was right

I guess he wanted me
to figure out my own way
make my own choice
decide what must be done

whatever I
had done.

Some questions can't be
answered—those are
the best ones: I could
imagine him saying that.

Answers, he would say,
are not a door to be shut
on a perfectly tidy room
but are more like a seed

waiting to sprout on
fertile ground, ready to
expand and unfold and,
one day, bloom,

poised to beget more
questions, deep within,

that might root out
the real answers.
He wanted me to
learn how to think for myself.

I guess that's
what he wanted.
He never answered
that question, either.

The Fall

we fall

we take a fall
we stumble
we trip
we fall forward
we fall back
on our sides
our bellies
our backs
our knees
our hands

we fall magnificently
clumsily
skillfully
awkwardly
dangerously
forcefully
softly
gracefully

we fall with
our eyes open
our eyes shut

or halfway in between

we fall standing up
walking
remaining still
climbing stairs
hiking a mountain
sliding down a slope

we fall stepping
dancing
running
racing
jumping
carrying laundry
      down the stairs

we fall laughing
crying
widening our eyes
in shock or surprise

we fall unknowingly

we fall to rise or
crawl or fall
again

we fall in line
fall out
fall into money
in and out of love
into being
on hard times
outside the perimeter

we fall once
twice
a thousand times

life is a dozen handfuls
of horizontal

falls

The Night a House Burned Down

The bread did not rise
as it should have but
looks more like a brown brick
of inedible grossness.
We were going to have toast
this morning, but now
there's only a rock.

This is the beginning
of a brick-like day.

An early email from
the school principal
told parents a
kindergarten teacher
died last night
in a fire.

A fire.
My kindergarten son asked me
about fire on the walk to school.
How do people die in a fire? he said.
There are so many ways,
but I don't know which
I should choose. He's only five.

I say what's easy: Sometimes
people can't get out of
their homes in time.
And he runs ahead
to his brothers,
satisfied for now.

It was more than a fire.
They're not telling the kids this,
but it was a disturbed husband,
who tied her up, shot her,
and set the house on fire.
These details will come later,
when I will think and brood
and endlessly question:

> What might he have done
> to all those kindergarteners
> if he'd come to school for a visit?

The hallway of my sons' school
is heavy, almost oppressive
with fear and sadness,
though no one cries where
we can see it as we pass through.
There is weeping in
the heaviness, however,
and I turn my face away

where no one can see my tears.
I did not know her, really,
just saw her in the halls
of my kids' school.
Just said hello when she
talked to my twins.
Just moved on by,
took life—living—for granted.

The hallways are emptier, too.
Some parents kept their children
home so they would not have
to talk about death
in their classrooms.
Some children already know,
and, rather than speak,
they look toward the
end of the hallway,
for their teacher,
back from the dead.
Some children hear, feel, see
the somber hush and
instinctively know
they should be quiet.

What is the measure of a life?
She taught for more than

sixteen years. How many
students remember her?
How many students' lives
were changed because of her?
Is it enough to remember
that she loved sunflowers,
the color purple,
and wearing flip flops?
How does a five-year-old
honor her memory,
remember her forever?
Will she be forgotten?

Will we all, one day,
be forgotten?

We should take some
sunflowers to school,
my first grader said
this morning.
He knew her, too.
They were her favorite.
So we did.

Life has petals.
When all of them drop
and the flower becomes a husk,

what remains is buried
and perhaps remembered
every year on
her birthday.

Regret

Regret is a solid thing
but not really:

        regret

brims at the lip
showing itself when you're
not looking at it

in shadows shifting
off to the corner
of your gaze: it

        is

pitch
        dark

you can't see any face
unless you're not looking:

        regret

takes shape slowly
like a crater blown in the ground

curling at the

                edges

like a bowl of dust
waiting to be
stirred

like a sizable hole

that holds all the things
a person did wrong

over all the days in all

                lives;

regret is a shifty thing
blowing in on a new wind

in specks and clots
riding the sunshine rays
that reach in from windows

like a call to

                banish

all wrongdoing,
as though it is so simple

like a layer of filth
that gathers without notice
until it's an inch thick

and weighing down a heart:
regret is a useless thing
unless a person can use

it

to do better and learn

and try to find the good:
if one can, essentially,

stop regretting
that it happened
and be glad it did

Happiness

happiness can be
a dangerous pursuit

no one really wants
to choose "evil," you know

it's just that sometimes a person
can glance at that "evil" thing

and it looks so attractive to them
that they start to believe

it holds their happiness
however crooked its fingers

they start to believe
the lies it tells—

that a person will find
fulfillment and love and respect

if a person walks
its way

and I'm telling you,

that one "evil" thing

that didn't feel so evil
in the first place

can start a whole
cascade of consequences

and at the end of it
a person will stand

in the middle of her life
choking spluttering reeling

and wonder what
the hell happened.

So why would a person
chase happiness at all?

Is that
a fair question?

The Maze

Life is a series of mazes
through which we feel our way—

we'll walk blind for a time
and then come upon a clearing

where everything makes sense
and everything feels easy

and after a while we'll move again
into the narrowed passageways

or dank alleys
of confusion

and feel as though we will
never be done with them

but passageways and alleys
come to an end sooner or later,

and then we will happen upon a door.
We will walk through the door,

and it will close behind us,

and there is nowhere to go but forward,

through the confusion,
walking ourselves to clarity

walking ourselves
home.

Life is a series of mazes
through which we feel our way.

Accident

Two lanes,
yellow line,
one crosses,
the other smashes.

What happens when
metal meets metal
on a two-lane highway
and no one's around
to hear it?
Does it sound like
the world collapsing
in on itself?
Does the world then
grow silent after the
initial cracking and squealing
that rang out—or didn't—into
the steely spring sky,
their songs silenced forever?

A bird flaps over the wreckage,
twitters unaffectedly,
and flies on its way,
the only movement
for miles around

in the now-quiet desert.

The Past

Forget it.
Forgive and
be done with it.
You get to choose
what you remember,
so just choose not to remember
the painful parts.

It's not as simple as all that.
I mean, who among you
was shoved in a closet
for an innocent game of
hide and seek and it turned out
the dirty old man who offered
to help you count to thirty,
because you weren't old enough
to even do that, wanted to only
play the seek part, because
he had a thing for little girls
and you couldn't see the truth
in his eyes, because he was a man
and you didn't have a man in your life,
only an overworked mother,
so you didn't quite know
how to distrust or fear

And how many of you
have carried a baby—two of them—
for twenty whole weeks,
almost to the safe zone,
only to have them break free from
the womb, the size of your palm,
while you watched in horrified
silence as they scratched and clawed
for breath, just enough of a breath
so they would live another day
or hour or minutes (they didn't)?
How many of you have buried
a baby in the smallest casket
you've ever seen—smaller than
a casket should ever be?
How many of you have had
to make the decision to cremate
your twin boys and put those ashes
in a tiny pot that sits on
a shelf in your living room?
How many of you have had
to pay the hospital bill for
a delivery and birth that did not
result in a child who now sleeps
in a home nursery you'd
already set up, because

she was so long awaited?

How many of you
have had to watch a father dying
the slowest kind of death,
from alcohol and cigarettes
and the devastating effects of guilt,
a father who left you when
you were right on the cusp of
becoming a woman and so
the things you carried became
everlasting things that you still
fight off and wade through today,
so your feelings about his dying
are a bag of tricks, mostly—
sadness, some days, because
you never quite got the chance
to make it right; anger, because
he died before he could find
the courage to make it right,
to become a real father
to his grown daughter;
sadness again, because a
of all you missed;
anger again, because
of all he made you miss—
over and over again.

It's not so easy to forgive
and forget the past when
these are the sorts of memories
you have. But it's not so much
the forgetting that matters.
What matters more is
coming to terms with the past,
understanding that it is part
of what made you,
believing that all wounds
can be stitched, though
they leave scars.

It takes strength
and resilience to hold tight
to a memory, to never let it
slip away, to write over
its destruction:
Redeemed.
Remembered.
Released.

Daydreams

Some say don't you dare

>let those eyes glaze over
>let that mind wander
>let the world slip away
>so you can imagine a new one
>in its place

what is a life
that is filled with dreaming
and how does one live now
if one is always living
in another then

>where is the joy
>in existing in another
>reality?

they say these problems
of the world are not solved
in starry-eyed dreams
nor are relationships forged
when we are not here, really

>so sit up

        pay attention
        keep your mind here
        make sure you don't miss a thing
        there is not a moment worth missing

after all
dreams
die

        Well maybe it's true
        that dreams all die one day
        and maybe it's true
        that I'll miss a little living now
        and maybe it's true that

the world's problems aren't
solved in starry-eyed wonderings
and daily dallying in
the expanse of a mind
but I'd sure like to try

        So I'll give you my dreams

Life

The petals fall:
the wind twirls them toward blades
that bend and straighten,

        a world off-center

It is a hatchet:
information, unwanted
It will change everything

        a future unmade

And yet:
in the hollowed out, exhumed earth
a seed opens, a bloom unfolds

        a brilliant reminder:

Life unmakes
and remakes
in quick succession

About the Author

Rachel is the author of six poetry books, *This is How You Know*, *Life: a definition of terms*, *The Book of Uncommon Hours*, *Textbook of an Ordinary Life*, *This is How You Fly*, and *Sincerely Yours*; a middle grade novel in verse, *The Colors of the Rain*, and a middle grade fantasy novel, *The Woods*; and multiple essay collections as well as books for children under a pen name. She has been writing poetry since the time she could hold a pencil and form what passed for letters on the page. Her first introduction to poetry was the brilliance of Shel Silverstein, whom she still reads today. She recently exposed her sons to the hilarious Jack Prelutsky poem, "Homework! Oh Homework!" which was one of her favorites as a kid. They loved it (as she still does).

Her poems for children and adults can be read in literary magazines and online publications around the world.

Rachel lives with her husband and six sons in San Antonio, Texas. She daily reads poetry (as well as many, many books) to her children, because poetry, she says, contains the essence of life, and reading, she says, is the gateway to a future of promise.

Author's Note

My dear reader,

Feeling stuck in an invisible, parenthetical life is not an easy place to be. It's not even a little bit enjoyable most days. If you are anything like me, you cannot wait to get out of it as soon as you possibly can. But I speak from experience: A parenthetical life has so much to teach us, if we let it. So, rather than wish ourselves out, I hope we (most days) choose to live our parenthetical life well.

Please don't forget to leave a review and share this book with your friends. Reviews help other readers know whether this is a book they'd like to have on their shelves, and when we share books with friends, we are giving authors one of the greatest gifts we can give: a word-of-mouth recommendation. A writer is indebted to those who pass along their book with a genuine "You should read this."

May you always live whole and blissfully free.

In love,
Rachel

Acknowledgments

How to thank all of the people who stand behind a writer and form their stairway to publishing? It's difficult, but I'll try.

I am so very grateful to:

Ben: Thank you for clearing for me the time and space to pursue my writing and for brainstorming with me and listening to my never-ending complaints about how hard it is and for never letting me forget why I do it.

Jadon, Asa, Hosea, Boaz, Zadok, and Asher: If you only knew how lovely it's been to be your mother during these parenthetical years. Stop growing up so fast.

Mom: What can I say that I haven't already said? Thank you for working so hard to give your kids what they needed. Thank you for being there. Thank you for loving us in spite of the ways we made it difficult. Thank you for teaching us that we matter.

My readers: You are wonderfully kind in your constant encouragement and your faithful reading.

God: My divine inspiration, my ultimate encourager, my

miracle time-creator. Thank you for this gift. May I use it well and for good, always.

Enjoy more titles from Rachel Toalson

racheltoalson.com

Rachel Toalson Poetry
Starter Library

Enjoy more of Rachel Toalson's poetry with these free downloads.

*To get your FREE books, visit ***
RachelToalson.com/FreeBook

*Must be 13 or older to be eligible